HOMES SWEET HOMES

HOMES SWEET HOMES

BY
OSBERT LANCASTER

Illustrated by the Author

———————

LONDON

JOHN MURRAY, ALBEMARLE STREET, W1

First Edition	.	.	November 1939
Reprinted	.	.	November 1939
Reprinted	.	.	January 1940
Reprinted	.	.	September 1941
Reprinted	.	.	January 1944
Reprinted	.	.	August 1946
Reprinted	.	.	August 1948

Made and Printed in Great Britain by Butler & Tanner Ltd., Frome and London

To
MY MOTHER

CONTENTS

PREFACE

THE poor benighted foreigner, so we are frequently and authoritatively informed, has no word for home, and although one may occasionally wonder why, in that case, the sentimental German spends so much time singing about his *Heimat* and his *Heimatsland*, it is not for us to question what has long since become an article of national faith. Assuredly the word does more work in one language than most do in six ; it serves, among other duties, to distinguish a psychological type—"homeloving" ; a high degree of discomfort—"home comforts," a standard of moral values—"there's no place like it," a noticeable lack of physical charm—"homely" ; and a radio programme of outstanding boredom—B.B.C. Home Service. But despite this tremendous adjectival expansion it still retains, beneath layer after layer of the treacliest sentiment, its original substantive meaning of the house in which one lives.

On closer investigation one is able to isolate the proper application of the word "home" still further, and properly confine it to the inside of one's house. At first sight this may appear sheer pedantry, but on reflection one comes to realize that the word implies a sphere over which the individual has complete control ; hence its enormous popularity in a land of rugged individualists. And whereas the appearance of the interior of one's house is the outcome of one's own personal tastes, prejudices and bank balance, the outside in ninety-nine cases out of a hundred is the expression of the views on architecture of a speculative builder, a luxury flat magnate, or even occasionally an eighteenth-century country gentleman.

Having thus established the extremely personal nature of home the author is left with an uneasy feeling that his present work may be thought to constitute a gross and ill-mannered violation of traditional privacy. To criticize the outward appearance of other people's houses is an act which needs no justification ; the public, of which he is a member, is forced to look at them whether it wants to or not, and he may even bamboozle himself into thinking that he is performing a public service. But to become the literary counterpart of the pertinacious salesman, or the too conscientious Air Raid Warden and storm the Englishman's castle, that is a very different kettle of fish. He therefore wishes it to be clearly understood that the present work is in no way one of criticism but rather of pure disinterested scientific investigation. Clinical detachment has been his constant aim and he has striven throughout to examine and classify each piece of chintz, each gas-bracket with the high-souled, unswerving rectitude of Pasteur contemplating the more revolting varieties of streptococci.

9

All over Europe the lights are going out, oil-lamps, gas-mantles, electroliers, olde Tudor lanthorns, standards and wall-brackets, and whether or not they go on again in our time, the present moment seems as good as any in which to contemplate the rooms they have illuminated in the past. For the history of the home provides the most intimate, and in some ways the most reliable, picture of the growth and development of European culture ; at all periods the average man (or for that matter the abnormal man) has revealed most clearly his prejudices, his standards and his general outlook in the ordering of his most intimate surroundings. In decoration no less than in literature *le style c'est l'homme même ;* and for self-revelation, whether it be a Tudor villa on the by-pass or a bomb-proof châlet at Berchtesgaden, there's no place like home.

That being the case the author, while being naturally anxious lest any claim of his should be judged even slightly exaggerated, feels compelled to abandon all false modesty and point out that the present work is nothing less than an exhaustive history of European civilization from the earliest times until the present day. Less gloomy in its outlook than Spengler, more circumspect in its treatment of questionable themes than Lecky and taking up far less room than either, he trusts that the present volume will provide profitable instruction during those long winter evenings when home is found to be indisputably best owing to the fact that both east and west are shrouded in perpetual and dangerous blackness. And if he should be wrong, then the reader by a mere flick of the wrist can save fuel and insure this work a fitting end by using it to keep those home fires, to which the author has devoted so much careful research, patriotically burning.

IT used once to be the fashion, when discussing the domestic architecture of the Normans, to stress, with a certain degree of high-minded relish, the considerable sacrifice of comfort in the interests of security. "Those vast walls, three foot thick, those slits of windows, that damp unhealthy moat, what a fearful testimony they provide" a previous generation of social historians were wont to exclaim, " of the unappeasable bellicosity of our rude forefathers ! " To-day, while still agreeing whole-heartedly with these conclusions, one finds it more difficult, as one peers through the lattice work of sticky paper across the window at the sandbags and corrugated iron in the next-door garden, to maintain the happy note of cultured superiority.

Nevertheless it remains perfectly true that the Normans were forced by the prevailing insecurity to live in small isolated communities protected, from the irridentist tendencies of the Anglo-Saxon peasantry and the too easily aroused enmity of their fellow-barons, by outworks and bastions the size and thickness of which inevitably reduced the living space. Thus in the majority of castles there was one communal living-room and one only, the Great Hall, in which the lord and his higher retainers lived, ate, and slept. In a few of the more elaborate examples there were one or two sleeping apartments hollowed out of the thickness of the wall for the ladies of the household. In all cases, however, the lower servants slept in the stables.

However intolerable such a state of affairs may seem to us, given the conditions of the eleventh century, this architecture was purely functional. And, moreover, in at least one case it retains its function in the twentieth, for was it not recently announced that the presence of a large castle in the centre of one of the principal cities of Wales, hitherto retained and treasured for antiquarian reasons, has now saved the town council large sums in the provision of air raid shelters ?

DURING the Middle Ages the original Spartan simplicity of the Norman home suffered progressive modification, and if no very high degree of comfort was finally attained, at the end of the period the houses of the rich compared very favourably with, say, the average first-class waiting-room in a modern provincial railway station.

In the course of time increasing security from internal disturbance led to the gradual abandonment of all but the most modest fortifications—a carp-stocked moat and a few token battlements—so that it was possible to increase both the number and size of the rooms. Nevertheless the hall retained its old importance and the majority of the household continued to spend most of their time beneath its now rather more elaborate and considerably larger roof.

A taste for privacy, however, was beginning to emerge and in the wealthier homes the master and mistress, and occasionally their children, had small bedrooms of their own and there was frequently a parlour, called a solar, in which the ladies of the house were accustomed to occupy themselves between meals. At the same time the upper classes began to interest themselves in the question of decoration and the plain white-washed walls of their Norman ancestors were hidden behind tapestries, painted canvas or frescoes according to the financial resources of the house-holder. In most houses the hall was still heated by means of a brazier in the middle of the room, the smoke from which was optimistically assumed to disappear through a hole in the ceiling, and it was not until the very end of the Middle Ages that the fire-place and chimney became anything like general, even among the well-to-do. Needless to say when this novelty first appeared it was roundly attacked by the conservative on moral grounds ; the comparative absence of smoke secured by this new device was bitterly regretted by all those, and they were as numerous then as now, who clung to the old English belief that if a thing is unpleasant it is automatically good for you. An immediate and shameful weakening in the moral fibre of the nation was confidently predicted.

Apart from these few improvements the home life of the period was much the same as it had been in Norman times. Glass was still very rare and the wooden lattices, which appeared at this date, let in considerably more wind than light and the floor was covered with rushes which were changed at the most infrequent intervals,—an unhappy arrangement since, as in all English country houses at every period, there were far too many dogs.

THE coming of the Tudors coincided with the beginnings of the Renaissance, but not for a long time was visible in England anything more than the first faint flicker of the dawn that in Italy had already ended the long nightmare of the Middle Ages. Thus the Tudor home in its fittings and furniture was only a rather more elaborate version of that inhabited by the previous three generations. The timber-work supporting the roof became ever more complex but the construction remained the same in principle ; tapestry shared the honour of being the most fashionable wall-covering with carved panelling ; and although carpets were imported from the East in larger numbers, they were still used as table coverings and wall decorations and never as carpets. However, the number of rooms increased rapidly and although the great hall still retained its importance, it tended to be reserved for meals and ceremonial occasions instead of being used as the general living-room for the whole household day in and day out. But towards the end of the period political events were the indirect cause of a considerable alteration in the generally accepted plan of a gentleman's mansion.

When Henry VIII dissolved the monasteries he presented their buildings to those whom he considered the most deserving of his friends and who thereupon set about converting them into country seats. Now throughout the Middle Ages the standard of comfort and convenience in the religious establishments, with the exception perhaps of such strict orders as the Carthusians who had never abandoned their original austerity, had been far higher than that prevailing in even the most palatial private house ; moreover, the number and size of the principal rooms was, of course, far greater. The result was that the English nobility and gentry suddenly acquired a taste for size and grandeur in their residences that they never subsequently lost.

However, it must be admitted that in the process of conversion the average monastery lost much of its original comfort and practically all its convenience, but the desire for such things remained and flourished, and enlightened persons such as Erasmus started bitterly to complain about the general untidiness, beastliness and smelliness of the average English home

B

QUEEN ELIZABETH'S grandfather was Lord Mayor of London and the immediate ancestry of the majority of her nobility was, from the point of view of the College of Heralds, even less memorable. In fact the Elizabethans were, almost to a man, *nouveaux riches* ; and in the decoration of their homes they employed all those symbols of recently acquired culture with a heartiness and an abandon which, when displayed by more recent generations, have seldom failed to provoke the polite merriment of the cultured readers of *Punch*. The typical figure of that golden age was not, it is sobering to reflect, the dashing cloak-flinging figure of historical fiction, but none other than our old friend Sir Gorgeous Midas.

In the home the immediate effect of this change-over in the seats of the mighty was to produce an atmosphere of oppressive and overwhelming richness. The comparatively simple linen-fold panelling of Tudor times gave way to acres of wood-work carved and chiselled with patterns of quite staggering complication and hideousness ; no sooner had a more plentiful supply of glass led to the installation of larger and more numerous windows than a rich gloom was at once brought back by the practice of filling every window-pane with dubious heraldry ; and although new methods of construction rendered unnecessary the presence of those pendant nodules so beloved of the builders of fan vaults and hammer-beam roofs, their place was promptly taken by clusters of disturbing and quite unnecessary plaster stalactites. Decoration for decoration's sake was the motto of the Elizabethans and every available inch of wall, ceiling and furniture was covered with lozenges, strap-work, heraldry and all the as yet completely undigested classical bric-à-brac of the Italian Renaissance.

However, in one respect at least the period marked an advance. Although the decoration of the Elizabethan house was in no way an improvement on that of the previous generation, the plan was markedly superior. The great hall while retaining its central position loses much of its former importance and at meal-times the family now abandon its draughty wastes to the steward and upper servants in favour of the cosier if less impressive winter-parlour. Moreover, the appearance of a grand staircase in addition to one or two of the old circular variety renders the first floor both more accessible and more popular, and it is at once further enriched by the presence of a long gallery, an impressive apartment used for exercise on wet days and the display of numerous paintings of well-dressed but frequently mythical ancestors.

NO great change of style marks the division between the reigns of Elizabeth and her cousin James, and in the realm of interior decoration the passage of time is only indicated by a progressive and welcome simplification. The new nobility were slowly becoming accustomed to their rôle and were no longer so conscious of the need to mark their transition into the ranks of the upper-classes by an overwhelming display of real wealth and bogus heraldry. As a result the average Jacobean interior is not, save in the region of the fireplace, quite so oppressively a background against which the contemporary woodcarver and plasterer can display unhindered their grisly talents. Moreover, although the average local builder's understanding of the four orders and other elements of classical architecture, which he acquired from cheap text-books translated from the Italian, remained shaky in the extreme, there is evidence of a growing mastery. The proportions are still almost invariably wrong but they are not quite so wrong as they had been formerly.

However, if no very drastic change is to be detected in the decoration of the house itself in the matter of furniture, the Jacobeans displayed a praise-worthy spirit of invention. Hitherto the well-dressed man had always worn well-padded breeches attaining, in the last years of Queen Elizabeth's reign, quite staggering dimensions ; now suddenly these went out of fashion and for the first time he was in a position to appreciate the painful disadvantages of the plain wooden chair. As a result the stuffing was now transferred from the sitter's backside to the chair he sat on, and upholstered furniture was introduced for the first time to a grateful public. Needless to say such luxuries were confined to the very rich, and for many years to come the less sensitive bottoms of the lower orders continued to rest on hard wood.

The style loosely described as Jacobean remained popular, with slight modifications, until the Restoration, but nevertheless as early as the reign of James the direction in which English domestic architecture was logi-cally to develop had been firmly indicated. When Inigo Jones built the Queen's house at Greenwich the Middle Ages were brought to an end and the English Renaissance, which was to find its highest expression in the architecture, decoration and furnishing of the home, had begun.

WITH the return of Charles II to his kingdom there opened a period which, decoratively speaking, lasted until the middle of the nineteenth century. A period in which continuous changes and improvements took place, but changes and improvements that developed naturally and progressively one from another and were the result of no sudden break with tradition. During the Commonwealth England had enjoyed a state of almost complete artistic stagnation, but there now arose in the person of Sir Christopher Wren an architect ideally fitted to continue the work started by Inigo Jones a generation before. Moreover the long exile abroad of the King and court led to the introduction of foreign, particularly French, modes, and fashion becomes of almost equal importance with convenience in the arrangement of the home. Now for the first time there appears upon the scene the smart and mondaine figure of the interior decorator.

The great fire of London made possible the speedy development of the town house proper ; hitherto it had been for the rich merely a country mansion which chanced to be in a town and for the poor a conglomeration of rooms over a shop jutting ever farther into the street. Now the genius of Wren devised a plan for London houses which, in essentials, remained unchanged until the coming of the flat. At street level a small entrance hall, a dining-room and a parlour ; on the first floor a large state room and principal bedroom ; above more bedrooms and closets and below ground that rather unfortunate device, the basement kitchen, that had been introduced from Italy at the end of the sixteenth century. The beauty of this plan lay in the fact that it could be modified or enlarged to suit almost all pockets and every variety of site.

The interior walls are still covered with panelling but the panels themselves are of good proportions and fewer in number ; moreover the aggravating gap between the ceiling and the woodwork is now banished and the cornice appears in the proper place. Monotony is avoided by the employment of richly carved mouldings and all that jungle of inefficient woodcarving is replaced by a few festoons of very naturalistic fruit, confined usually to the fire-place and the panels immediately above it. The whole effect is, perhaps, rather heavy but at least it is a well-proportioned heaviness.

ALTHOUGH the *Grande Monarque* was by no means alone among his royal namesakes in lending his name and number to a style of decoration (to be pronounced in a superior interior decorator's accent " louiscatorse ") he at least bore a considerable amount of the responsibility for the style so called. The great palace of Versailles was the fruit of his own inspiration and every inch of the decoration bore in some degree the impress of his personality, and as Versailles was immediately copied in every country in Europe and continued to provide the model for the perfect palace so long as palaces continued to be built, he can perhaps claim to have had as much influence in interior decoration as any other single individual. For although very few people are actually called upon to live in palaces a very large number are unwilling to admit the fact and so a style devised for the further glory of a seventeenth-century French monarch has been eagerly adopted from time to time not only by other royalties great and small but also by English noblemen, Jewish business men, South African diamond kings, American millionaires and film-stars of all nations.

In England during the seventeenth century there was on the whole too little money to encourage the accumulation of those vast mirror-bedecked, satin-hung, generously gilded suites of enormous rooms, but in one respect the example of the builder of Versailles was eagerly followed with direct results in the sphere of interior decoration. The habit of receiving in bed, so popular with both sexes among the very wealthy and important, led to that apartment being decorated with uncommon luxury and pomp. The walls beneath a heavily gilded and carved cornice were hung with damask of a colour and pattern to correspond with the bed curtains. The ceiling, divided into variously shaped panels by heavy mouldings, was prettily enlivened with a variety of cleverly painted rapes ; and the general interest of the apartment was still further increased by a liberal supply of pictures, Susannah and the Elders, Samson and Delilah, Judith with the head of Holofernes and other such subjects, in which a certain popular appeal was judiciously balanced by the warrant of Holy Scripture.

A TASTE for the grandiose, like a taste for morphia, is, once it has been fully acquired, difficult to keep within limits, and all the various potentates who during the first decades of the eighteenth century so eagerly followed where Louis XIV had led, soon found themselves provided with residences which, while being undoubtedly of an extreme impressiveness, fulfilled just about as many of the ordinary requirements of a home as do the Pyramids. Seldom have architects achieved dwellings further removed from the definition of a house as *une machine à habiter* than such masterpieces as Wurzburg, the Winter Palace, Zabern and Blenheim. Ceilings only incidentally fulfilled their usual rôle of covering a room ; their primary purpose was now to provide a background for the athletic amours of Jupiter and other inhabitants of Olympus cleverly and lovingly depicted by Tiepolo, Lebrun or Verrio. Pillars and columns might possibly support an arch or cornice but were just as likely to be employed for their decorative value alone. Staircases no longer took the shortest route from one floor to another but writhed and curled in every direction—vast processional ways designed for the passage of half the Almanach de Gotha in full war-paint—and every inch of available wall-space was covered with trophies, busts, caryatids and escutcheons in marble, malachite, gilt, plaster and shell-work.

This state of affairs could not, of course, last for long. Few of his fellow-sovereigns enjoyed the robust health of the Sun King and the enormous discomfort of living in these glittering barracks, which not all the ingenuity of science nor all the wealth of the Indies could warm, and in which the dining-room might be anything from a hundred yards to a quarter of a mile from the kitchens, soon drove them to build smaller, though scarcely less luxurious, residences in the parks attached to their main palaces. But nevertheless this passing passion for pomp and glory at all costs was not without its effect on the art of decoration. The main staircase then acquired an importance which it never subsequently lost, and the taste for long vanishing vistas of columns and arches led to the introduction of the *tromp d'oeil* whereby the desired effect could be obtained at a quarter the cost and which retained its popularity as a method of wall-decoration for many years to come. Above all, the decorative artist then acquired a freedom and an increased power of invention without which the rococo style of the next generation could never have been devised.

THE great triumph of the architects and decorators of the Rococo period was the discovery of a way to reconcile the demands of fashion and comfort. The invention, skill and virtuosity of their predecessors of the baroque have seldom been surpassed but, as has already been pointed out, their masterpieces rarely achieved that indefinable air of cosiness, of being *chez soi*, a desire for which must from time to time assail all but the most robust megalomaniacs. Now there was developed a style of decoration in which most of the familiar motives of baroque reappear but are treated with a lightness and a freedom which renders them admirably suited for the decoration of apartments conceived on a less heroic scale. The old division of the wall into panels is retained but the lines of the mouldings lose their former stiffness and are broken into curves, or garlanded with flowers or terminate in elaborate scrolls or shell-work. Chairs, mirrors, picture-frames—all lose their old arbitrary shapes, and the cornice over a door may dissolve before one's eyes into a mountainous oriental landscape, or a pediment blossom forth into a bundle of corn tied up with ribbons. Obviously this could become unbearably tiresome and boring, but such was the sureness of taste of the masters of this style, so consummate their control of their material, that in nine cases out of ten such pitfalls were widely avoided.

It would, however, be a mistake to assume that rococo was a hard and fast style which only flourished for one short period; it is far rather a way of feeling, a mood which may recur in any sufficiently sophisticated epoch. After its popularity had declined on the continent it suddenly reappears once more in England and produces the Brighton Pavilion. During the Victorian era it vanishes from sight (although it left its mark in the decoration of those *papier-maché* and mother-of-pearl trays and boxes so popular in the early years of that reign) only to re-emerge again at the very end of the century and find a deplorable expression in Art Nouveau. To-day, unashamedly derivative, it enjoys a fresh vogue in the work of Messrs. Whistler and Messel. But never has it achieved such triumphs as it did in the mid-eighteenth century, when its sudden blossoming coincided with the maturity of such master craftsmen as Pöppelman, Cuvillies and Chippendale.

IN England comparatively few homes, and those only of the very rich and smart, reflected even faintly the glitter of the baroque and rococo fireworks sent up by the contemporary continental designers. The average English room during the first half of the century was simply a logical development of the Restoration apartment evolved by Wren and his followers. As time went on the mouldings and cornices became lighter and the introduction of new woods, such as mahogany, produced a greater variety of panelling, but the chief advance was displayed not so much in the decoration of the room itself but in the furniture it contained. Formerly this had been very restricted in quantity and almost standardized in design, but now an innumerable supply of objects began to accumulate in various corners, owing their introduction not to their utility but solely to their decorative value. An ever-increasing supply of porcelain, coming at first from the Far East and later from the factories at Bow and Chelsea, invaded the mantelpiece and eventually demanded special glass fronted cupboards for its accommodation and display. Niches had to be made to shelter the busts of Roman worthies which the antiquarian enthusiasm of Lord Burlington and the Dilettanti unearthed from the soil of Italy in suspiciously large quantities. And the tireless industry of Augustan poets and High Church divines rendered the presence of numerous large book-cases essential for the proper equipment of a gentleman's home.

These innovations were for the most part the reflection of the master's taste and sensibility, but along with them others that indicated feminine influence were now introduced into the decorative field. While panelling, painted or plain, remained the most popular form of wall covering in such masculine apartments as the library and dining-room, in the bedrooms and boudoir its place was being taken by wall-papers, usually imported from China, and silk and satin hangings.

Moreover, there was one field in which the rococo spirit proved as fertile in invention in this country as in France or Germany—that of Chinoiserie. The china and paper coming in large quantities from the East proved a powerful source of inspiration to our designers and from now until almost the end of the century there flowed a constant stream of furniture, plasterwork and painted panelling all of which embodied Chinese motives, and in the treatment of which contemporary craftsmen, above all Chippendale, displayed a taste and invention in no way inferior to those which found expression in the pavilions of Potsdam and Nymphenburg.

THE main, in fact the only, influence in English architecture from the seventeenth century onwards had been classic ; Italian classic with Inigo Jones, French and Dutch classic with Wren and his followers, Italian once more with Lord Burlington and Kent. Now another foreign fashion arises, still classic, but totally different from the foregoing modes. This time it is the decorative art of antiquity itself, as revealed by the excavations at Herculaneum and later Pompeii, that brightens the walls and ceilings of Mayfair. This development might quite easily have ended in disaster, for the whole movement was surrounded with a vast amount of donnish pedantry and expertise ; moreover, the taste of ancient Rome as displayed at Pompeii is strongly suggestive of Tottenham Court Road ; but fortunately at that moment there arose a new generation of architects and designers, headed by the brothers Adam, whose genius enabled them to take this unpromising material and evolve from it a style which remains one of the greatest glories of the applied arts in this country.

With enormous skill the urns, sphinxes, vine leaves and all the rest of the boring bric-à-brac of the first century of our era are now moulded in plaster, ormolu and other materials, painted, gilded and rearranged on candelabra and mirrors, on friezes and cornices in such a way as to achieve the most varied yet homogeneous scheme of decoration. At the same time panelling disappears from the walls which are painted in plain flat colours with narrow bands of moulding outlining plain areas of varying shapes but invariably excellent proportions. Great attention is lavished on the ceiling on which ovals and lunettes painted with antique scenes by the talented Miss Kauffman are surrounded by an elaborate geometrical tracery of gilded plaster. On the floor, as like as not, is a specially woven carpet reproducing the pattern overhead. Over the doors entablatures and cornices of an impeccable correctness support busts and urns while the blank spaces on the walls are enlivened by medallions.

It is at this time that the supremacy of the interior decorator is finally asserted. Hitherto this profession, developed if not invented by Kent, had, while not being altogether unlucrative, scarcely attained the dimensions of a full-time job. Now the brothers Adam (incidentally far better decorators than architects) established it firmly on that smart and fashionable plane on which to-day so many bright young men and shrewd old women so profitably operate.

THE artistic enthusiasm of the polite world having once been directed towards antiquity showed no signs of abating. Rather did it become more intense with time and tended to concentrate on ever earlier phases of civilization. Thus the Pompeian was soon superseded in the popular favour by the Etruscan, which in its turn was swept aside by the Greek, which last maintained its sway unchallenged save by the Egyptian, for a brief period immediately following Napoleon's eastern campaign, for close on half a century.

This new passion for antiquity reached its highest pitch in France where it became indissolubly connected first with the French Revolution and secondly with Napoleon. It is therefore the first example which history affords us of an ideological style ; that is to say a style adopted not so much for its own beauty or convenience but rather for the sake of the political qualities of the civilization that first evolved it. Certainly no style had ever proved so all-embracing. Architecture, furniture, painting, women's dress, military uniforms all approximated as closely as possible to what were piously hoped to be antique models. Luckily, however, very little Greek furniture had survived the centuries so that designers were forced to use their own imagination and that soulless mechanical copying which is the bane of all revivals was very largely avoided.

In England that robust national common sense, which had not yet been sapped by the Romantic movement, saved us from the more ridiculous excesses of *le style Empire* and a very pleasant and serviceable style of decoration was evolved in which these new neo-Greek fantasies were skilfully grafted on to the old, trustworthy eighteenth-century stem. At the same time the exuberant and artistically dominating character of the Regent himself led to a more lavish display of gilding and more dashing use of colour. Formerly blues and greens in pastel shades were most commonly employed but now such assertive tints as terra-cotta and maroon spread themselves over the walls, while for curtains and upholstery sulphur yellow, royal blue and crimson generously sown with wreaths, stars, cornucopias, lyres and sphinxes were used with the most resolute self-confidence. Full-blooded yet intellectual, aristocratic and at the same time slightly vulgar, the Regency style was sufficiently paradoxical to be perfectly in tune with the age which gave it birth and to lend some shred of justification to its popularity to-day.

THE early Victorian or, as some purists prefer to call it, the Adelaide style, while it undoubtedly marks a decline (the elegance of the Georgian and the vitality of the Regency have both departed), nevertheless represents not unworthily the last phase of a great tradition. The lines are heavier, the decoration coarser, yet the proportions are still good and there is a general atmosphere of solidity and comfort. Painted walls now vanish, not to reappear for nearly a century, beneath a variety of patterned papers, striped, spotted and flowered. Mahogany reigns almost supreme as the popular wood for furniture, though both birch and rosewood maintain a certain vogue. Carpets are either elaborately floral in pink and white or severely patterned in billiard-cloth green or scarlet. Fire-places are comparatively plain in marble.

However, it is not so much the quality of the individual furnishings that has altered but the quantity. Now for the first time the part tends to become more important than the whole and the room assumes the function of a museum of *objets d'art*. The mantelpiece is transformed into a parade ground for the perpetual marshalling of rows of Bristol glass candlesticks, Sèvres vases, Bohemian lustres around the glass-protected focal point of a massively allegorical clock. For the better display of whole cavalry divisions of plunging bronze equestrians, Covent Gardens of wax fruit, bales of Berlin woolwork, the drawing room, the library and the boudoir are forced to accommodate inumerable cupboards, consoles and occasional tables. The large family portrait loses none of its popularity but the fashion for miniatures and silhouettes enables the range of visible reminders of the importance of family ties to be extended to the third and fourth generation of uncles, aunts and cousins of every degree.

Futile as such generalizations invariably are, one may perhaps hazard a suggestion that nothing so markedly distinguished the average Victorian from other generations as this passion for tangible evidence of past emotions ; a longing to recapture in some concrete form the pleasure of a visit to Carlsbad or Margate, the unbearable poignancy of Aunt Sophia's death-bed. Hence the unbounded popularity of the memento, the *Reiseandenken*, and the keepsake. Harmless and rather touching as such a fashion may be, the intrusion of this aggressively personal note into decoration led to future trouble when it became necessary to find without fail a prominent place for such a surrealist variety of objects as a sand-filled paper-weight from Alum Bay, a lock of little Willy's hair and dear Fido, stuffed and mounted.

"Little bits of porcelain,
Little sticks of Boule
Harmonize with Venuses
Of the Flemish school."

Financier's Song (mid-nineteenth century).

THE Victorian passion for symbols, so essentially charming and domestic in its origins, soon proved capable of considerable expansion. If room could be found for an endless collection of objects whose sole justification was sentimental, then there was ample accommodation available for concrete reminders, not of happy moments of the householder's past, but of the satisfactory state of his financial present. *Objets d'art et de vertu* had been collected by rich men since the end of the seventeenth century ; but, in the majority of cases, for their own sake ; now they are feverishly sought after for the kudos they acquire for their owners and as visible evidence of enormous wealth. In order properly to display these hoards of Dutch pictures, Italian marbles, German glass and what-have-you, a style was evolved which combined all the richest elements of those which had preceded it and which soon became standardized throughout Europe. The heavy golden cornices, the damask hung walls, the fringed and tasselled curtains of Genoese velvet, the marble and the parquet were as rich and as inevitable in the wealthiest circles of Vienna as they were in London, and formed almost the official background for the flashy pageant of the Second Empire.

Nothing in this style, which we have named Rothschild after what was, until recently, its finest existing example in this country—the old Rothschild house in Piccadilly, was new save the gasoliers : and the only original element was a fondness for the recent past which displayed itself in a taste for the more lavishly gilded examples of Louis Quinze furniture (hitherto each succeeding generation had surveyed the styles of its predecessors with the utmost distaste and when Empire furniture came in Chippendale went out to join the Sheraton and the Queen Anne in the servants hall). Nevertheless, despite this ample evidence of cultural insufficiency, one is forced to admit, if like Henry James one " can stand a lot of gilt," that it was a style that at least possessed the courage of its opulent convictions.

THE official religion of Victorian England is usually considered to have been an evangelical form of Christianity suitably modified to bring it into harmony with a public school education and the principles of free trade, but one is sometimes tempted to wonder whether in large tracts of the country, particularly in Scotland, an older faith that blended ancestor worship with totemism did not reassert its hold on the upper classes from about the 'fifties onwards. How else can we explain the sudden appearance of those vast, castellated barracks faithfully mimicking all the least attractive features of the English home at the most uncomfortable period of its development, and filled with rank upon rank of grim-visaged, elaborately kilted forebears? What other explanation can be found for the presence of these enormous necropolitan menageries stuffed full of stags and caribou, bears and tigers—creatures which, however attractive in life, in death perform no function but the constant employment of legions of housemaids with dusters? What other reason can be advanced for the phenomenal popularity of Mr. Landseer whose only merit as a painter was the tireless accuracy with which he recorded the more revoltingly sentimental aspects of the woolier mammals?

Whether or not Scottish Baronial has its origins in primitive religion its popularity was soon assured in all classes of society. Tartan, stags' heads and faithful representations of Highland cattle in various media soon enlivened the Coburg simplicity of the Court as successfully as they added to the discomfort of cosy little villas in Tulse Hill or Twickenham where the rafters were unlikely ever to ring with the sound of the pipes. And to-day many a dusty hotel lounge, many a dentist's waiting-room with their ritual display of these old symbols, recall, like the mosques of Spain, the former domination of a vanished faith.

WHILE the drawing-room, boudoir and bedroom of the average Victorian house might from time to time undergo the most extraordinary metamorphoses, the dining-room retained almost unaltered the character it had acquired at the very beginning of the period until, in many cases, the war of 1914. It seems as though the Victorians while willing to tolerate frivolous decorative experiments in those less important apartments were not for one moment prepared to allow any light-hearted tampering with a shrine sacred to the important processes of mastication and digestion. Moreover, not only was the dining-room safe from purely temporal changes but also from those arising from personal idiosyncrasies so that its form and decoration were practically standardized throughout the upper and middle classes.

The table, sideboard and chairs were invariably of mahogany and of a sufficiently massive construction safely to support the respective weights of the serried rows of decanters and side dishes, the monumental *épergnes*, and the diners themselves. The wall-paper was always dark and nine times out of ten of a self-patterned crimson design ; that colour being considered, quite rightly, as stimulating to the appetite. The carpet was invariably a fine Turkey.

Conventions no less rigid governed the choice of pictures. These, if they were not ancestral portraits, had either to be still-lives or landscapes and in both cases the choice of subject was sternly restricted. If they were still-lives they must be those vast pyramids of foodstuffs in which the red of the lobster strikes so bold a note of colour, beloved of the Dutch School ; if landscapes, then storms at sea, Highland cattle or forests of a fearful gloom. (The only permissible exceptions to this depressing range were scenes in the Holy Land and then only if depicted at sunset.) Late in the period conversation pieces were allowed provided the personnel were carousing Cardinals. Generally speaking the only alternative to oil-paintings as a form of wall decoration were steel engravings, preferably by Mons. Doré, of sacred subjects. (It should never be forgotten that the dining-room of the period had taken over some of the functions of a private chapel in that it was invariably the scene of family prayers.)

So lasting were these traditions that the childhood memories of many still comparatively young retain their ineffaceable impress. Thus the sight of a Van der Velde seascape still brings the taste of mulligatawny whistling up from the author's sub-conscious while the flavour of Bordeaux pigeon summons with all the completeness of Proust's tea-soaked madeleine an unforgettable cloud of Mons. Doré's angels hovering over the Colosseum.

FROM the beginning of Queen Victoria's reign until the early 'seventies the decorative arts had undergone little modification ; details became slowly coarser, colours ever more garish and after the great Exhibition of 1851 this process of gradual decline was much accelerated, though there were no signs of any drastic change. But now a variety of strange breezes sprang up from several directions at once which in combination succeeded in blowing the stuffy yet cosy atmosphere of the average Victorian interior to oblivion.

Hitherto the Pre-Raphaelites had been an obscure artistic clique unknown to the majority of the public, but suddenly their practices and doctrines attained a new prominence and soon all the female inhabitants of such artistic neighbourhoods as Chelsea and South Kensington developed a strange, goitrous affliction of the throat and the cheerful magentas and sulphur yellows were banished from their homes in favour of sage green, peacock blue and every variety of ochre. At the same time the fervent mediaevalism, that had been flourishing architecturally since the beginning of the century, under the influence of William Morris (the best of whose wallpapers were the only legacy of any artistic value bequeathed us by the whole movement) developed a philosophic-cum-economic tinge which found its final expression in the Arts-and-Crafts movement. Curiously enough alongside this revived Gothicism there sprang up a reaction in favour of the classicism of Queen Anne which was responsible for Pont Street,[1] and which led to a hasty dash being made to the attics to rescue whatever had survived in the way of early eighteenth-century furniture.

Unfortunately the contemporary culture had hardly had time to digest these diverse and revolutionary influences when a new and even more disastrous treasure-house of art was discovered in the Far East. Soon the Blessed Damozel was yearning down from between pendant Japanese fans ; the cast-iron mantelpiece, tastefully incised with sun-flowers by Mr. Walter Crane, supported two Chinese ginger-jars and a vase of Satsuma ware in which a solitary lily bore witness to the high regard in which the oriental ideals of flower arrangement were now held ; and the Queen Anne furniture, so lately restored to the drawing-room, had to share the honours with chairs and sofas whose spiky frailty was assumed to be oriental in inspiration if not in actual origin. Surrounded by such testimonies to her sensibility as these the intellectual young woman could safely relax and lend a properly appreciative ear to the patter of Pater and whispers of Wilde.

[1] See *Pillar to Post*.

THE cult of æstheticism (some of the effects of which we have considered a few pages back), though flourishing in the 'seventies, was only accepted whole-heartedly by a comparatively small section of the population—the *haute Bohème* of the day. But in the following decade it penetrated in a modified and truncated form into every drawing-room in the land. Needless to say its better features, such as the wall-papers of William Morris and its theoretical insistence on simplicity, never achieved more than a very limited popularity, whereas the blue china, the Japanese gewgaws and the spindly furniture received a rapturous welcome in every home from Tulse Hill to Belsize Park. However, it must not be supposed that the new arrivals dispossessed any of the existing ornaments ; room was found for all and the artistic little snuff-bottle from Yokohama shared a corner of the mantelpiece (now tastefully draped with fringed green plush) with the shell-work light-house from Shanklin.

It was not long before these treasures were joined on their already perilously over-crowded ledges by a new wave of invaders (the whole process is one which inevitably calls to mind the constant penetration of the Picts and the Celts and the Jutes and the Angles and practically dictates the employment of ethnographical jargon) and, by the end of the century, the problem of *lebensraum* had become acute. These new-comers were a tribe of china shepherds and shepherdesses hailing from a strange Kate Greenaway-cum-Marcus Stone conception of the eighteenth century— examples of a now extinct school of plastic art, a few specimens of which are still occasionally to be found, for some inexplicable reason, in the windows of old-fashioned dairies.

But perhaps the most striking feature of the period is the extraordinary love of plant-life which manifests itself in every interior. Aspidistras, palms, rubber-plants and every variety of fern thrive and flourish on all sides, while, no longer living but still decorative, the bull-rush disputes with the pampas grass the possession of the costliest available vase. Dimly through the jungle half-light one perceives on the walls, in very wide gold mounts, the exquisite water-colours of Mr. Birket Foster and many talented studies of irises and other artistic flowers by the young lady of the house. And when the gas is turned up and all the myriad green leaves, swaying in time to the strains of Balfe or of Tosti cast strange shadows on the chrysanthemum-covered wall, one would fancy oneself in some tropical fairyland as yet unpenetrated by the dauntless Doctor Livingstone.

THERE was one type of interior which, although its distribution was always far more limited, rivalled in persistence the Victorian dining-room,—namely the masculine apartment known as the study, or more familiarly the den, of which many examples are still to be found in schools, colleges, and country vicarages differing, hardly at all in furniture and decoration from those in which professors, divines and ecclesiologists laboured and reflected when the Gothic Revival was still young. It was never a style that one would find in every house ; only in the homes of public-school men of a studious type. It had as little attraction for Ouida's guardsmen and W. S. Gilbert's æsthetes as it has for their descendants to-day, but nevertheless it may perhaps be thought to represent, as does no other Victorian style, all that was best in that great age. The prevailing atmosphere of high thinking and plain living, of *mens sana in corpore sano*, may be a trifle oppressive, but it is balanced by an undeniable air of comfort.

The details are almost invariably the same and must be familiar to many of my readers—and perhaps painfully so, for when in youth one heard that dread summons " You will come and see me in my study after chapel," it was always to an apartment such as this that one was bidden. The Gothic grate behind its club fender, the groups of long vanished rugger players beside the pipe-rack on the mantelpiece, the Arundel prints in their ecclesiastical mounts hanging between the faded sepia photographs of Greek temples and Swiss mountains, the Gothic book-case with its dusty rows of Paley's Evidences and the brown-backed volumes of the Badminton library,—all these are changeless and inevitable. Likewise the little marble model of the leaning tower of Pisa, the lump of stone from the Acropolis, the whiskered ecclesiastics in Oxford frames and the large bow window looking on a garden dark with laurels.

To-day such isolated examples as exist represent, like those ruined temples in the jungles of Yucatan that are said still to be tended by some last uncomprehending survivors of the old Maya priesthood, the final dying outposts of a vanished culture. But they can still on occasion arouse a powerful nostalgia in the breasts of all but the most hard-boiled.

D

AS the old Queen's reign drew to a close, the eighteenth-century note in interior decoration became more marked. In smart circles the thin spindly chairs in shiny black wood, etched with little gold lines, that had been so popular in the 'eighties were gradually replaced by pseudo-Hepplewhite creations in rose-wood and satin wood. With the arrival of the South African millionaires, the style Rothschild, which had always proclaimed itself eighteenth century in inspiration, enjoyed a new lease of life and numerous needy cabinet makers and French polishers were kept busy preparing a fresh supply of genuine Louis Seize furniture. At the same time fireplaces ceased to provide a riot of artistic tiling and tended to be " after Adam." And the potters of Dresden found ample employment in the large-scale manufacture of bewigged and hooped figurines, of an archness that the eighteenth century would have found overwhelming.

However, it must not be imagined that this new passion for the styles of Louis Seize et Quinze produced any fundamental change in the appearance of the average drawing-room. The jackdaw strain inherent in every true Victorian, which led to the constant acquisition of innumerable objects of dubious virtue, was stronger than ever, and the crowded ranks of knick-knacks received numerous additions. The new-born consciousness of our Imperial destiny led to an influx of native handiwork from every quarter of the globe—interesting little plaster statuettes of Indian servants, brass trays from Benares, cedar-wood boxes and tables of every size and shape, lavishly inlaid with mother-of-pearl—while an increase in the size of photographs brought innumerable aunts and uncles, dim royalties and dimmer generals from out the decent obscurity of the family album and scattered them in heavy silver frames all over the room. To accommodate all these new-comers, as well as the original inhabitants, the mantelpiece soon proved quite inadequate, and in order to cope with what were rapidly becoming slum conditions that interesting structure the overmantel was devised, which not only served to relieve congestion but also provided an admirable opportunity for the skilled wood-carver to do his ingenious worst.

On the walls the exquisite productions of Lord Leighton and Sir Lawrence Alma Tadema still enjoyed pride of place, and it was not until the very end of the century that a revived interest in the works of Greuze led to their gradual removal, first to the spare room, then to the bathroom landing and finally to the servants' hall.

APART from *Art Nouveau*, of which the vogue was mercifully but not unnaturally limited, the main decorative influence in Edwardian period was French. And just as the dining-room was the key apartment of the Victorian era, and the studio of the immediately post-war decade, so the boudoir, significantly enough, was the characteristic region of the house in this silver age of European culture. This French influence took the familiar mid-eighteenth-century form, but with a wholehearted-ness that produced what almost amounted to a full-dress rococo revival. Walls were once more divided into damask-filled panels ; ceilings and cornices came out in a rash of plasterwork ; gilt easels groaned beneath the burden of untrustworthy Greuzes and dubious Bouchers ; and the floor was always covered with what was piously hoped to be an Aubusson. A legion of little ornaments still required a quantity of occasional tables for their accommodation but now tended to fall into two categories—the admittedly precious and the supposedly functional. In the former were included all the usual knick-knacks, with the addition of as many specimens of the ingenious Mons. Fabergé's costly handiwork as the owner could afford, while the latter embraced a large variety of musical instru-ments, which might or might not be played, and such happy symbols of the alliance of art and industry as lamp-supporting bronze nudes and voluptuous nereids twined round ink-pots. At the same time the stream of silver-framed photographs attained the dimensions of a flood engulfing every piece of furniture in the room. A particularly happy idea for the display of these tokens of family affection or social grandeur was to scatter them wholesale among the palms and other potted plants of a suitable robustness, which still retained all their old popularity. Thus one could frequently espy many a tiara'd dowager or bemedalled hussar peeping, jaguar like, from beneath the tropical undergrowth, while in all the best houses from the most prominent branch a pouchy and familiar eye, separated by a well-kept beard from a glossy expanse of waistcoat across which a con-descending hand had scrawled " Edward R.", surveyed the world with a glance of slightly baleful *bonhomie.*

THE imminence of the twentieth century produced among thoughtful and artistic people a feeling that the new era, which was confidently hoped would be one of unexampled peace and progress and which the cultured and businesslike French were already preparing to usher in with yet another Exposition Universelle, should be provided with a suitably modern style of decoration. Such a style, it was generally considered, should clearly and unequivocally mark a break with the immediate past and therefore the plainer it was the greater would be the contrast. Fortunately the foundations of such a style were ready to hand; ever since the 'eighties in the byways of Chelsea and the lost valleys of the Cotswolds a handful of devoted Artists and Craftsmen had been living the simple life according to the doctrines of William Morris, surrounded by hand-woven linens, vegetable dyed, and plain unstained oak furniture by " goode workmen wel ywrought."

At first, while the control of the movement remained in English hands, something of the original simplicity was still maintained, albeit a remarkably self-conscious and uncomfortable simplicity; but once the eager designers of Paris and Munich got their hands on it the result was nightmare. And as soon as the English decorators realized that at last this country had produced a style that had at once earned the approbation of the continent they too cast restraint to the winds. In less than no time a tangle of water-lilies cast their tenuous roots from ceiling to floor; chairs, tables, mantelpieces, as though they had swallowed the White Rabbit's potion, shot skywards with a rapidity that rivalled Alice's; in letters of a tortuous and illegible craftiness suitable mottoes, punctuated with tiny hearts, were beaten on copper and incised with pokers on wood; and hand-made pots of an assymetrical bulbousness that rendered them entirely useless for any practical purpose supported with difficulty a spray of honesty or a single iris. Here and there on the walls were displayed a few of the rare pictures which could possibly compete with the decoration; Japanese prints the size of postage stamps in mounts like table-cloths, a Beardsley drawing or two and possibly a Whistler nocturne.

So extraordinary a style requires some explanation and it may not be too fanciful to assume the existence of a recurrent passion for tortuous curves and sinuous lines deeply embedded in the sub-conscious of the European artist, which from time to time finds expression in such exoticisms as the flamboyant Gothic of the later Middle Ages, mid-eighteenth-century rococo and, most deplorably, in *Art Nouveau*. Certainly no style seems at first glance to provide a richer field for the investigations of Herr Freud.

TO-DAY the epithet Edwardian has perhaps acquired, thanks to Miss Sackville West's charmingly expressed nostalgia, and the prodigious memoir-writing feats of the surviving Edwardians, a rather too exclusively aristocratic application. Its syllables summon up for most of us a confused vision of electric broughams, the portraits of Laszlo and Sargent, Patti in Manon, Homburg and Miss Cornwallis West. In fact this glorious vision, in so far as it corresponds in any degree with reality, is illumined by the after-glow of the Victorian era while the cheerful rays of the new dawn (subsequently discovered to be false) with which the majority of Edwardians considered the reign to have been ushered in, fall on a totally different collection of symbols.

Large areas of shiny white paint, masking the mahogany dear to the previous generation ; sticky-looking but cheerful chintzes patterned with large cabbage roses on a white background ; the beautiful and moving pictures of Herr Böcklin, made available to a large public through the commercial acumen of the Berlin Photographic Company ; these, together with the early plays of Mr. Shaw and the novels of Mr. Meredith, were some of the more characteristic signs of the times. But in addition there was one trait, which found ample expression in the contemporary interior, that particularly distinguishes the Edwardians from their immediate forbears— their pathetic faith in the benefits of science.

Soon the home was invaded by an entirely new collection of furniture and fittings in the design of most of which the supporters of *Art Nouveau*, by no means yet moribund, had secured an unfortunate monopoly. From the heart of a tinted glass flower at the end of a terrifyingly sinuous brass stalk there now peeped the electric light bulb, while in the fireplace a strange collection of stalactites, in a black lead sarcophagus embossed with a design of water lilies, glowed with gas-produced heat. Pendent from the wall a complicated contraption of vulcanite, mahogany and polished brass carried the householder's voice, at the mere turning of a handle, to such of his neighbours as were similarly equipped, while the hanging book-case, itself a striking testimony to little Willy's skill with that popular scientific toy the fret-saw, groaned beneath its load of Mr. Wells's marvellous romances. Everything in the garden, to use a contemporary phrase, was lovely.

And then one day the largest and most impressive miracle of modern science hit an iceberg in mid-Atlantic, and the prevailing optimism received a shock which two years later was repeated on a scale and at a length sufficient to banish it for ever.

THE post-war era, from the social historian's point of view, started some time previous to that fatal afternoon at Serajevo. The truth of this tiresomely paradoxical statement is borne out by the number of phenomena that we have come to regard as particularly characteristic of the roaring 'twenties which were, in fact, flourishing in the first two years of his late Majesty's reign. Female emancipation, jazz, bright young people, large-scale labour disputes, cubism, the gowns of Mons. Poiret, Diaghilev's Russian Ballet, all made their first appearance in a world in which any existing war-weariness dated from the Boer War.

Of all these startling and varied developments by far the most important in the realm of interior decoration was undoubtedly the last. So far-reaching were the changes that this remarkable theatrical venture brought about in the drawing-rooms of the great world that Napoleon's conquest of Egypt (which also littered the *salons* of London and Paris with boat-loads of exotic bric-à-brac) provides the only possible, although inadequate, parallel. Before one could say Nijinsky the pale pastel shades which had reigned supreme on the walls of Mayfair for almost two decades were replaced by a riot of barbaric hues—jade green, purple, every variety of crimson and scarlet, and, above all, orange. Gone were the Hubert Roberts and the Conder fans and their place was taken by the costume designs of Bakst and the theatre scenes of Benois. The Orient came once more into its own and the piano was draped with Chinese shawls, the divan replaced the chaise-longue and no mantelpiece was complete without its Buddha.

Not the least of the Russian Ballets achievements was the social kudos it acquired for art. Throughout the nineteenth century the aristocracy had displayed an ever-increasing dislike of culture (such æsthetic movements as those of the 'seventies and 'eighties flourished far more abundantly in the neighbourhood of the Cromwell Road than round about Park Lane), but now Art came once more to roost among the duchesses, where it was at length productive of a wave of modified Bohemianism. This produced a tendency to regard a room not so much as a place to live in, but as a setting for a party, with the result that the studio (so easy to run in a time of acute servant shortage) was suddenly much in demand for purely residential purposes.

Significantly enough, that happy acceptance of the wonders of science, which had been such a feature of the Edwardian age, vanished along with the flowered chintzes and the overmantel, and the electric light now took refuge in an old Chinese temple lantern and the telephone lurked coyly beneath the capacious skirts of a Russian peasant doll, dressed after a design by Goncharova.

WHILE the drawing-rooms of the upper and middle classes under-went a variety of changes in the years between the Great Exhibition and the General Strike, the decoration of the average cottage remained very much the same, and even now, in the age of cheap furniture on the instalment plan and functional flats for the proletariat, there still exist in remote districts a few specimens, as yet untenanted by intel-lectuals, in which the old style is still worthily displayed.

Against a waxed wall-paper, dark in hue and boldly floral in design, are ranged innumerable ornaments and pictures, for the true cottager still retains that passion for objects, which the cultured have so signally abandoned. Oleographs of deceased sovereigns and the late Lord Roberts, comic cats with the arms of Weston-super-Mare lavishly emblazoned on their buttocks, photographic mementoes of long forgotten bean-feasts jostle one another on the bobble-fringed mantelpiece, while among the numerous trophies of rod and gun, artistically mounted, and hand-tinted camera studies of the dear deceased, the flower entwined Gothic lettering of some pithy saying from the scriptures strikes a welcome note of lettered piety. And on the round central table and the window-sill a striking collection of potted ferns testifies to a natural interest in horticulture.

Soon, if our left-wing housing experts have their way, such interiors will have vanished for ever. The small tight-shut windows, the light from which is further dimmed by a barrage of Nottingham lace and a Maginot line of potted plants, will be replaced by a wide expanse of hygienic vita glass admitting buckets of light and air, even though the agricultural labourer, who has usually had his fill of both commodities during his day's work, might perhaps prefer the shuttered gloom which he is still in a few cases allowed to inhabit. The horsehair sofa must give place to a labour-saving, mass-produced arm-chair of chromium steel, and the hand painted view of Lyme Regis with the high lights picked out in mother-of-pearl will vanish in favour of a clever little camera study, taken from a most original angle, of Magnetogrosk. And the texts, which both in form and content are anyhow infinitely preferable to those poker-work exhortations to " take a cuppe of kindnesse for auld lang syne " and beaten copper reminders that a man's best friend is his dawg (beloved of the golf-playing classes) will then, presumably, have been transformed into such bracing slogans as " Religion is the opium of the people," in a functional type, for ideological reasons devoid of capitals.

IN earlier and less enlightened times the majority of cottages were inhabited by landworkers and a sprinkling of retired retainers spending the evening of their days in the modest rural comfort provided by the large-hearted nobility and gentry whom they had served. To-day this barbarous state of affairs has been almost completely abolished. Nine out of ten country cottages (that is, the more sanitary and comfortable nine) are occupied by writers, film stars, barristers, artists and B.B.C. announcers, and as a result the interior decoration of the average cottage has undergone considerable modification.

The flowered wall-paper, shiny with wax, has been replaced by hygienic distemper of an artistic pastel shade. The plastic souvenirs of famous seaside resorts are banished in favour of genuine examples of peasant handicrafts coming from Czecho-Slovakia by way of an interesting little shop, run by gentlefolk, in the Brompton Road. The oleographs and tinted camera studies have disappeared and their place is taken by hand-printed rhyme sheets, clever little woodcuts and expensive reproductions of those ubiquitous Sun-flowers. No longer is the Family Bible visible on a richly covered centre table ; instead " A Shropshire Lad " (hand-printed edition on rag paper, signed by the author and limited to two hundred copies), occupies an " accidentally " conspicuous position on an " artist designed " table of unstained oak.

However, so extraordinary are the workings of taste and fashion that in recent years there has been a return among the ultra-sophisticated to the genuine cottage interior ; but needless to say the aspidistra is worn with a difference. Photographs of late-Victorian wedding-groups return to the walls, but they owe their position not to any sudden excess of family feeling but to their allegedly humorous qualities. Similarly steel-engravings and wax fruit enjoy a come-back on an " amusing " basis. At first sight an extremely simple observer might imagine that the Victorians were back, but it would not be long before he realized that all these symbols are firmly displayed between inverted commas.

DURING the course of the first European war the eighteenth century, as a source of inspiration, was almost completely neglected. This was not altogether unnatural, for that golden age, still surrounded as it was by a happy haze of Edwardian wishful thinking which conveniently blurred its less attractive aspects, now appeared singularly remote from the unpleasant realities of war-time Europe. (People were apt to forget that the age of Crébillon and Fragonard was also the age of Frederick the Great and Maréchal Saxe.) Moreover, we were all still fighting to make the world safe for democracy—an ideal which would have exercised almost no appeal for the contemporaries of the Earl of Chatham. It was not surprising therefore that, in so far as the decorative arts continued to flourish, the exotic charms and barbaric colour schemes popularized by our gallant Russian allies reigned supreme.

Once the war was over, however, and it became obvious that the democracy for which we had striven was neither so safe nor so agreeable as many people had optimistically assumed, the aristocratic qualities, which eighteenth-century culture had so successfully embodied, soon regained their old appeal. But this new revival, owing largely to the writings of the talented brothers Sitwell, differed considerably from that which had flourished in Edwardian times. Now it was Italy, and to a lesser extent Spain and southern Germany, which provided the model. Gone were the Louis Seize chairs and the Largillière portraits, and their place was taken by innumerable pieces of hand-painted furniture from Venice and a surprisingly abundant supply of suspicious Canalettos. At the same time a markedly ecclesiastical note is struck by the forests of twisted baroque candlesticks, willingly surrendered by countless Italian padres (in exchange for the wherewithal with which to purchase up-to-date machine-turned brass electroliers), old leather-bound hymn-books cunningly hollowed out to receive cigarettes, and exuberant gilt *prie-dieux* ingeniously transformed into receptacles for gramophone records. And all the little Fabergé knick-knacks and Dresden china shepherdesses are finally routed by a noble army of martyrs from the Salzkammergut whose plaster writhings are rendered properly decorative by a liberal application of iridescent paint.

THE most remarkable development in urban domestic architecture during the inter-war period was undoubtedly the rapid popularization of the large block of flats. Hitherto the English, almost alone among European nations, had resolutely refused to become flat-minded, but during the 'twenties and 'thirties of the present century the acute shortage of domestic servants, the sedulous aping among all classes of everything American, the appalling rise in the rates and an increased familiarity with the works of Dr. Marie Stopes led to a wholesale abandonment of the capacious and dignified mansions which had been the pride of the upper and middle classes in Victorian times in favour of these labour-saving cliff dwellings which have done so much to ruin London's skyline and provide so gratifying and easy a test for the marksmanship of German bombers.

The modern flat falls into one or other of two categories ; either it is " self-contained " or it is " luxury." The first class (so called because it contains the owner's self and nothing else), is usually divided into a bed-sitting-room, a kitchenette (a word which reveals with sad clarity the state of modern culture) and a bathroom. It usually fulfils its claim of saving labour by being so abominably ill-planned that no respectable domestic can be induced to work in it. The luxury flat, on the other hand, with little or no more floor space than the self-contained variety, is divided up with fiendish ingenuity into a dining-room, drawing-room, lounge-hall, three bed, two bath, a kitchen and all the usual offices.

Apart from their planning both varieties have much in common. In each case the bathroom is by far the largest room in the flat, the walls are so thin that a radio on the ground floor is clearly audible at the top of the block, and such rooms as do not look out on to an interior well faced with glazed lavatory bricks invariably face the largest and busiest traffic thoroughfare in the immediate neighbourhood.

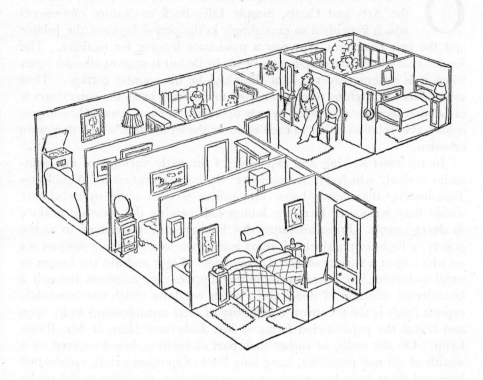

ONE of the less happy, but unfortunately more widespread, results of the Arts and Crafts, Simple Life, Back to Nature movements which flourished so exceedingly in the period between the Jubilee and the first European War was a passionate longing for rusticity. The Englishman's home need no longer be his castle but it must at all costs (even when it is within easy reach of the City) be his country cottage. Thus urban domestic architecture soon ceased to exist and in all the outer districts of London its place was taken by row upon row of rural retreats bearing no conceivable relation either to each other or the streets into which they were crowded.

In the most striking and expensive of the early varieties of this semi-rustic revival, which for convenience we have classified as Wimbledon Transitional,[1] the country-house atmosphere is even more overwhelming within than without. Here the lounge-hall reaches the ultimate peak of its development. From an impressive landing, always referred to as the gallery, a flight of polished oak stairs lead down to a gleaming parquet sea on which float a variety of rich Turkey rugs. Light and air, the former in small quantities, the latter in unlimited supplies, are admitted through a bewildering selection of doors and French windows which one constantly expects (such is the theatrical complexity of their arrangement) to fly open and reveal the pyjama-clad forms of Mr. Robertson Hare or Mr. Ralph Lynn. On the walls, or rather such part of them as is not covered by a wealth of old oak panelling, hang long lines of sporting prints, punctuated here and there by a barometer or a warming-pan, testifying to the strong sporting instincts of the squirearchy of Metroland.

Although in real life the popularity of this style of decoration has waned considerably of recent years, its predominance remains unchallenged in certain sections of the theatre owing to the fact that it provides an equally convenient setting for the gay philanderer on his amorous prowl from bed-room to bedroom and the third most dangerous man in Europe desperately trying to conceal the corpse of the Chinese butler before the end of Act II.

Needless to say this style, which first appeared in the early 1900's, is still regarded as the last word in up-to-date elegance in film circles where it provides the invariable background for all scenes of English high-life.

[1] See *Pillar to Post*

"Four postes round my bed,
  Oake beames overhead,
  Olde rugges on ye floor,
  No stockbroker could aske for more."

Sussex house-agents song.
(*Traditional, early twentieth century.*)

NOT even the first world war and its aftermath could sensibly diminish the antiquarian enthusiasm which had first gripped the English public early in Victoria's reign ; and the enormous advance in mass-production methods that took place during the inter-war period only served to increase the enormous output of handicrafts. The experience gained in aircraft and munition factories was soon being utilized in the manufacture of old oak beams, bottle-glass window-panes and wrought-iron Tudor lighting fixtures.

In interior decoration the cherished ideal, relentlessly and all too successfully pursued, was a glorified version of Anne Hathaway's cottage, with such modifications as were necessary to conform to transatlantic standards of plumbing. In construction the Tudor note was truly sounded : in the furnishing considerable deviations from strict period accuracy were permissible. Thus eighteenth-century four-posters, Regency samplers, and Victorian chintzes all soon came to be regarded as Tudor by adoption—at least in estate agency circles.

Soon certain classes of the community were in a position to pass their whole lives in one long Elizabethan day-dream ; spending their nights under high-pitched roofs and ancient eaves, their days in trekking from Tudor golf clubs to half-timbered cocktail bars, and their evenings in contemplating Mr. Laughton's robust interpretation of Henry VIII amid the Jacobean plasterwork of the Gloriana Palace.

The height of absurdity was finally reached shortly before the second world war when it was seriously proposed to build an exact reproduction—only naturally three times the size—of the original Globe theatre in Southwark to which patrons were to be ferried across the river in Elizabethan skiffs rowed by Elizabethan seamen.

STAUNCHLY as the neo-Tudor enthusiasts waged their olde-worlde campaign, they were never able completely to stifle the opinions of those who held that the brave new world of the 'twenties and 'thirties demanded a brave new style. Desperate efforts were made to convince the architectural public that half-timbering and leaded panes were easily adaptable to the requirements of nine-story blocks of flats, and that reinforced concrete methods of construction were ideally suited to support bigger and better beams ; but apart from one or two gargantuan luxury " Closes " the flat builders were disinclined to put these ideals into practice. They were therefore faced with the problem of evolving some style of interior decoration to harmonize with the bogus Hollywood modernism of the type of exterior which they preferred.

The resulting style was a nightmare amalgam of a variety of elements derived from several sources. The foundation was provided by that Jazz style that enjoyed a mercifully brief period of popularity in the immediate post-Versailles period, which was itself the fruit of a fearful union between the flashier side of Ballets Russes and a hopelessly vulgarized version of Cubism. To this were added elements derived from the *style coloniale* popularized by the Paris Exhibition of 1927, such as an all too generous use of the obscure and more hideous woods, and a half-hearted simplicity that derived from a complete misunderstanding of the ideals of the Corbuisier-Gropius school of architects and found uneasy expression in unvarnished wood and chromium plate, relentlessly misapplied.

It is significant that the old English fondness for disguising everything as something else now attained the dimensions of a serious pathological affliction. Gramophones masquerade as cocktail cabinets ; cocktail cabinets as book-cases ; radios lurk in tea-caddies and bronze nudes burst asunder at the waist-line to reveal cigarette lighters ; and nothing is what it seems. On reflection it is not perhaps surprising that disaster should have overtaken a generation which refused so consistently to look even the most ordinary facts in the face.

FROM the late eighteenth century onwards social distinctions had always been clearly distinguishable in interior decoration. On the one hand there existed the vast mass of middle and upper middle-class homes in which the décor and furnishings seldom underwent any sudden drastic change but were slowly and almost imperceptibly modified from generation to generation. On the other there were a small number of ultra-smart householders who reacted instantaneously to every change of fashion and whose houses seldom presented the same appearance two years running. It was the latter class of patron who adopted and popularized such styles as first Russian Ballet and Curzon St. Baroque. The most recent style to catch their fancy was Vogue Regency.

While there is little that one can say in favour of any attempt to re-create a vanished style in conditions totally different from those in which it first flourished, a revival of the decoration and furnishing tastes in favour in the first quarter of the last century has a rather more logical justification than most such antiquarian enthusiasms. The period between the Napoleonic wars and the upheavals of 1848 was like the inter-war period through which we have just passed—one in which vast social and political changes took place and which witnessed the final disappearance of the old eighteenth-century culture which was already in decline. Moreover, the Regency style represents the last development of the classical tradition that started with Inigo Jones. It was followed and obliterated by a series of irrational and disastrous experiments, the outcome of the enthusiasms aroused by the romantic movement working through the media all too generously provided by the Industrial Revolution. To-day the more sensible of modern architects realize that the desperate attempt to find a contemporary style can only succeed if the search starts at the point where Soane left off.

Luckily the furniture of the Regency period possesses in an exceptional degree the quality of adaptability—it " goes " as well with a strapping pink nude by Picasso as with the less generously proportioned nymphs of David or Etty. And a Recamier sofa is in no way embarrassed by the close proximity of a rug by Marian Dorn. So long, therefore, as no attempt is made to follow the fatal will-o'-the-wisp of period accuracy, Vogue Regency remains as suitable a style as any for a period in describing which the phrase Transitional, it is now apparent, is the grossest of understatements.

WE have seen how, throughout the nineteenth and early twentieth centuries, the average interior tended to become more and more crowded with furniture, ornaments and knick-knacks of every variety. It is not therefore surprising that at last a violent reaction should set in. The voice of the new Puritans, nourished on the doctrines of Gropius, Le Corbusier and Mumford, first attained a really authoritative ring in the late 'twenties, but even in the succeeding ten years, while it was listened to with ever-increasing respect, the number of persons who felt compelled to act upon such advice as it so generously gave remained disappointingly small. This apparent failure of the reformers in the realm of domestic architecture (in the shop, the factory and the hospital its triumph, though delayed, is inevitable) is, one fancies, one of psychology. The open plan, the mass-produced steel and plywood furniture, the uncompromising display of the structural elements, are all in theory perfectly logical, but in the home logic has always been at a discount. The vast majority, even including many readers of the *New Statesman*, crave their knick-knacks, though not in Victorian abundance, and are perfectly willing to pay the price in prolonged activities with broom and duster.

At the moment there are signs that many of the leaders of the school, though not of course the more strict, are compromising, and a selected assortment of *objets d'art et de vertu* are being once more admitted. At first sight they are a grim collection, but nevertheless they fulfil their old illogical function—the cactus sprouts where once flourished the aspidistra and the rubber-plant, the little bronze from Benin grimaces where smiled the shepherdess from Dresden, and in the place of honour formerly occupied by the kindly Labradors of Sir Edwin Landseer there now prance the tireless horses of Monsieur Chirico.

WHEN Monsieur Le Corbusier first propounded his theory of the house as *une machine à habiter* it may be doubted whether he foresaw the exact form in which it would be translated into fact. That other well-known architectural authority, Herr Hitler, must claim the credit for recent compliance on the part of the insular British with the extreme dictates of the continental functionalists. Here we see the bare bones of structure unconcealed save by a flood of interesting and stimulating instructions from the Town Council, the Home Office, the Head Warden, the Fire Brigade, old Uncle John Anderson and all. Here all attempt at applied decoration, apart from an occasional rude drawing of a pouchy-eyed, middle-aged paranoiac with a tooth-brush moustache (that is rapidly attaining a purely totemistic significance), has been abandoned and exclusive reliance is placed on the inherent decorative qualities of corrugated iron and unbleached canvas.

Whether or not enforced familiarity with this rugged décor over a prolonged period will in fact have any very marked effect on the average person's taste in interior decoration one cannot at the moment pretend to say. One thing, however, seems certain; after the first air-raid much of that enthusiasm for vast areas of plate-glass, which has been so marked a feature of the modern movement, will vanish for good.